This work is originally designed as a PEP (Personal Empowerment Process) Processor's handbooklet for use in group and individual sessions, however, its' format can indeed be used by anyone; including the Processee themselves.

The key premise of this PEP Booklet presses upon the truth that, nothing is truly forced on us in our life... but that instead EVERYTHING allots us at least two choices. Sometimes we don't recognize the choice(s) because we are blinded by our FEELings in the situation or simply are just too committed to our general way of THINKing.

This PEP Booklet will remind us and show in detail that NOT ONLY do *we all have choice(s)* in every situation and aspect of our lives, but what's more, that the choice selected is critical to the overall evolution of our consciousness leading towards realigning with our TrueSelf.

Health-Wealth-Happiness is our birthright, it's the very fabric of our being. Yet we find it so difficult to obtain and maintain. Why is that? It's because most do not truly innerstand what Health-Wealth-Happiness is, why it is and where it is.

In a world of billions of people, many of us still feel alone. And in our state of aloneness we find ourselves losing ourselves in loneliness.

There is a whole big world out there, and although we live in it, and move throughout it... we know at the highest recesses of our being that we are not a part of it.

Soon, because of this, we find ourselves in a state of mild or major depression. Nothing seems to fill the void we feel...

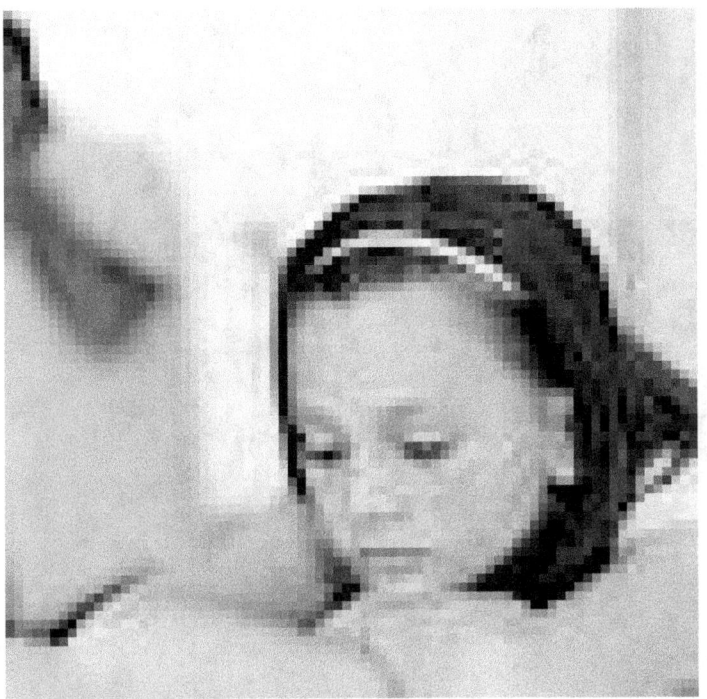

Not school, work, sports, activities, hobbies, games, foods, shopping, various us forms of entertainment...

Even our family, friends and loved one aren't enough...

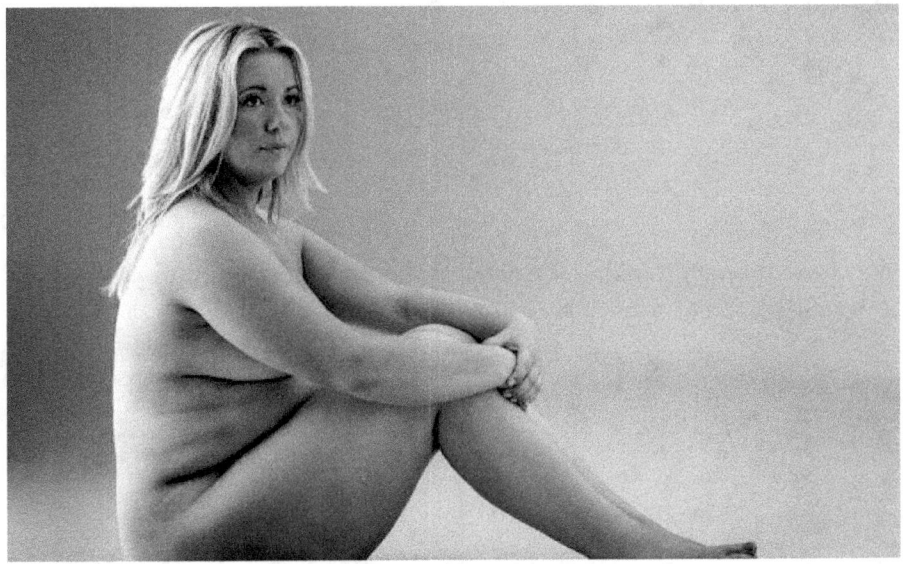

We become totally uncomfortable with who we are, our bodies, our height, weight, shape, our sexuality, etc. We feel vulnerable, naked and exposed in our FalseSELF.

We chase money, thinking it will solve the paradox of Health-Wealth-Happiness...

But... we find ourselves with only a portion of this illusion...

We then become slaves to our cyclic pursuit of such illusions...

We think that we can find it in intimate relationships...

Whether we put ourselves first or another, the results are the same...

We seek out joy in our interpersonal relationships, to no avail...

Even our family life cannot TRULY fulfill the void...

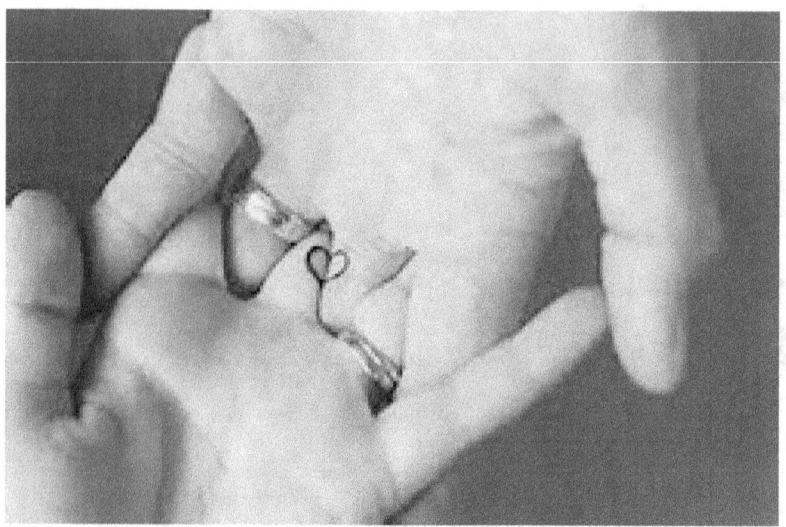

It is ONLY that when we attempt to hold on to things/people outside of ourselves, believing that they complete us, that we become dependent on finding synthetic temporary substitutes for our natural state of Health-Wealth-Happiness

Then we choose to wear a mask when interacting w others, because we don't know our TrueSelf and we hide behind the image of our FalseSELF... sometimes our mask pleases the other(s), sometimes it doesn't... but it leaves us feeling incomplete and drained.

We attempt to find joy in the shadow FalseSELF of who we really are. But it is ONLY a mirage.

At times a little light of knowledge of the TRUE PATH to Health-Wealth-Happiness shines in our lives, but we still remain lost in the shadow state of our FalseSELF...

In our shadow state of FalseSELF, we uselessly hope to form some real connection to others, yet they too are in their FalseSELF state...

So, in our desperation we begin to celebrate or exalt to ways of our FalseSELF and our connection with others in their FalseSELF

Many have promised us this truth, only to leave us more disappointed or confused then before... this is because they have shown us an untruth of what Health-Wealth-Happiness truly is and how we can really achieve it...

We have been taught to think of Health-Wealth-Happiness as three separate compartments...

Happiness, Health & Wealth
What you think about...you bring about.

We have been taught this formula out of its proper order.

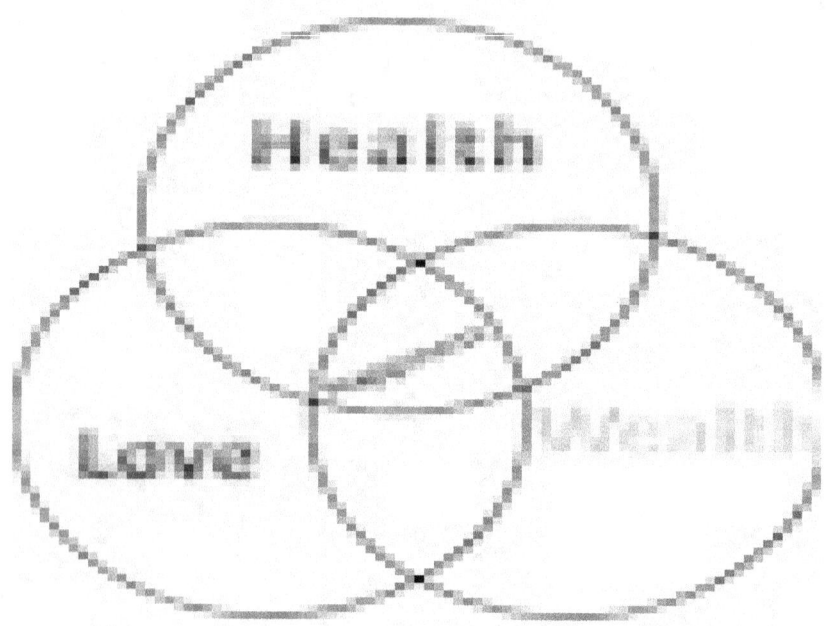

Indeed some have portrayed Health-Wealth-Happiness to be an interlocking triad... however, even in this near correct representation they till have given us incorrect sequences ...

Most sources infer that there are actually three separate key principles to unlocking the door to Health-Wealth-Happiness...

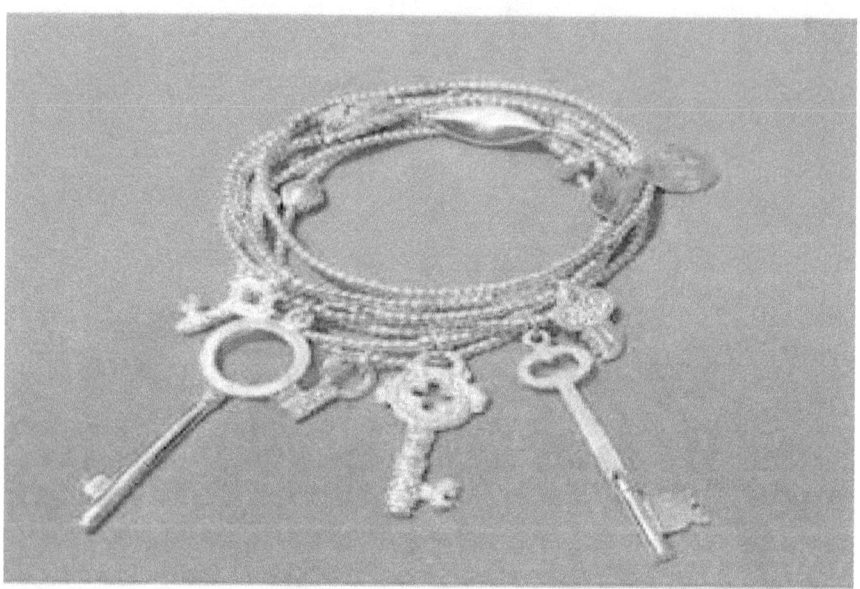

These same sources not only misguided us to believe that there are three separate key principles that unlock some mystical door to some a foreknown place containing Health-Wealth-Happiness, but what's more, that these three key principles are some exotic fancy complicated concepts or precepts...

But the truth is that there is **ONLY ONE door and thus there is but ONE KEY.**

This SINGLE KEY lies in the very nature and purpose of our being

Possessing this **SINGLE KEY** will allow our FalseSELF to receive the necessary energy/light that will lend to the realigning/awakening of our TrueSelf.

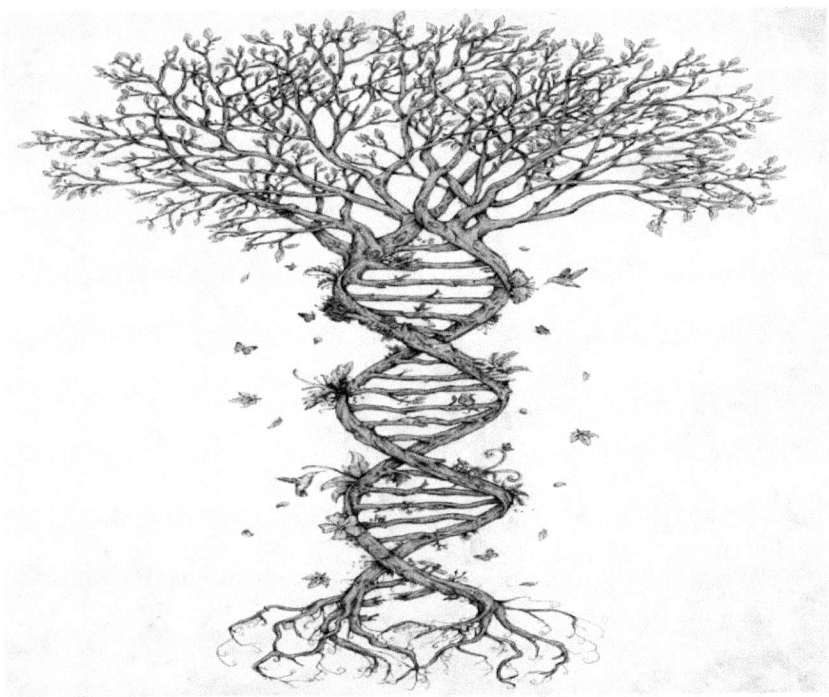

As **ENERGY REALIGNS US**, we will begin to grow from the core/root of our being, to the height of who we are truly meant to be...

As Energy/Light that is TRUTH begins to shine/work in our life, it will begin to realign us with our TrueSelf; which THE ONLY PLACE THAT HEALTH-WEALTH-HAPPINESS is.

This is where the true celebration of our life begins...

The magnificence of Energy, through its' threefold-state will transform you so wonderfully

As ENERGY begins to work into you,

Energy begins to work THROUGH YOU...

Energy begins to OUT OF YOU...

This is HOW ENERGY REALIGNS YOU!!!

This will reawaken your TrueSelf, allowing you to experience true Health-Wealth-Happiness.

Knowing now that it has always been with us… for we do not find Health-Wealth-Happiness, we define it.

Now we can truly rejoice in **HOW ENERGY REALIGNS US** with our TrueSelf, which the **ONLY PATH TO HEALTH-WEALTH-HAPPINESS...**

Once ENERGY REALIGNS YOU with your TrueSelf, you'll begin attracting others whom have also found their TrueSelves...

Then you find the connection that you have with others much more rewarding...

So, you can choose to learn **HOW ENERGY REALIGNS YOU**, to awaken your TrueSelf, and experience the **ONLY TRUE HEALTH-WEALTH-HAPPINESS** there is...

Or you can choose to remain struggling, buried in the endless pain of your FalseSELF...

IT'S YOUR CHOICE

THE DASOLAMI Institute

Daughters And Sons Of Light Advanced Metaphysics Industries

The New Perspective

We at **The DASOLAMI institute** hail from the premise that ALL human beings, are born with, and are meant to maintain throughout their entire life, a *perfected* state of **Health-Wealth-Happiness,** which we refer to as one's *TrueSelf*.

[Any state other than this we refer to as our *FalseSELF*].

Our goal at **The DASOLAMI institute** is to provide the *working conclusive Data*, which can then use as tools to realign oneSELF, thus returning them to their state of *TrueSelf*, where they will once again regain their naturally *perfected* state of **Health-Wealth-Happiness.**

The working *conclusive* Data outlines HOW ENERGY REALIGNS US with our *TrueSelf* state which is the source of all of our true **Health-Wealth-Happiness.** This PEP quite easy, if we only acknowledge a *basic scientific truth* and apply its THREE SIMPLE STEPS...

BASIC SCIENTIFIC TRUTH

ENERGY

Energy is BUT ONE THING... *never more*.

Energy is one thing that can express itself as an infinite amount of things/ways.

Just as you are ONE THING/PERSON that can express yourSELF in an infinite amount of ways.

Solar energy, radiation energy, mechanical energy, argon energy, light energy, thermodynamic energy, nuclear energy, etc, are ALL just different frequencies of The ONE AND ONLY energy that there is...

Called

TACHIYON

Everything in existence is but a frequency of ENERGY.

Energy is in CONSTANT MOTION, NEVER still/at rest.

Because Energy CONSTANTLY moves, it constantly vibrates.

Energy's continual vibration produces what is known as frequency.

Frequencies are the people, places and things in our [existence] life.

VIBRATION is the continuous movement of energy between 2 or more points. How fast this movement takes place is known as The Rate of Vibration.

FREQUENCY... Is produced by vibration. The rate/speed of the energy's movement determines the frequency that is produced. Everything except Energy is Frequency.

Energy IS

Energy DOES (vibrates/moves).

Energy HAPPENS (causes things to be)

This simple SCIENTIFIC TRUTH is paramount in the H.E.R.U (How Energy Realigns U/You) aspect of our DASOLAMII P.E.P (Personal Empowerment Process).

Once you innerstand this basic scientific truth, you can then begin to apply the Simple Step which allows Energy to realign you.

THE 3FOLD-STATE

T.A.B
(Thoughts, Attitude, Behavior)

T

Thought(s) ... (energy) What you think

A

Attitude(s) ... (Vibration) How you feel

B

Behavior(s) ... (frequency) How you act (thing you attract)

This is exactly how our TAB process works

Our Thoughts put us (our SELF) in a state called a vibration i.e, (Attitude/FEELing), which eventually (sooner or later) becomes our frequency (Behavior/ACTions).

Example:

You get up early THINKing "Today is going to be a bad day."

Eventually you're going to begin FEELing like it is a bad day.

Then you're going to begin ACTing like it is a bad day.

THOUGHT, ATTITUDE and **BEHAVIOR** erect what is known as a 3fold-state. This 3fold-state is EXTREMELY powerful, as it is a metaphysical arch ritual. Arch means the highest type. Ritual being the structured process of doing something to gain a specific result.

If your perception (Thought) is that everyone is out to get you, then it will APPEAR to you as though EVERYONE is out to get you. No matter if those people are 100% out to help you; you will only see what your perception is showing you.

This holds true for every Thought process of ours.

INNERSTANDING EMOTION

What is Emotion really?

Emotion is simply Energy in motion (moving) or Energy's Motion!!!

EMOTION

|

v

E-MOTION

|

v

Energy in MOTION

We remember from the earlier *conclusive data* that the motion or movement of Energy produces vibration... vibration determines frequency.

Emotion is just ENERGY MOVING ALONG THE FREQUENCY SPECTRUM (more about the frequency spectrum later).

Because there is ONLY ONE ENERGY, there is... ONLY ONE EMOTION.

WHAT???!!! < --------- (That's you. ☐)

I know, I know, I know, this Data "blows your mind", and leaves you like .... "Huh?" (< -- also you).

[But] bear with us, and I will [explain] it really simply, so that THIS ALL MAKES SENSE TO YOU.

What has misaligned us and continues to keep us that way is; the misinformation that has been programmed into our THOUGHTS, and allowed to become our ATTITUDE, until it becomes habitually modeled in our BEHAVIOR.

We have been programmed to THINK that...

- Emotion and feeling are the same.
- We have more than one emotion
- We can NOT control our emotion

Your former programming is ALL incorrect.

Emotion and FEELings are different!!!

WOW!!! (< --- you again) ☐

So, you wonder how does this outline the difference between EMotion and FEELing?

Easy.

EMOTION IS THE PROCESS
OF GETTING TO THE DESTINATION
(FEEL)ING IS THE DESTINATION ITSELF

- EMotion is Energy moving = Vibration
- FEELings are reached through Emotion/vibration = frequency

Everything that exists is but a specific frequency, except Energy

Energy is NOT frequency nor a frequency. The effect of Energy's vibration, causes all frequencies.

FEELings are the range of frequencies (things) caused by Energy's Motion (E-motion), which we can FEEL or experience.

The rate/speed of Energy's vibration determines the frequency that is caused. Energy's vibration is responsible for producing things. This is simple SCIENTIFIC TRUTH.

Everything vibrates at its specific rate/speed, producing an exacting frequency; which we call A Unique Energy Signature. We, ourselves, are a particular frequency. When we operate at our proper frequency, we experience alignment with our TrueSelf.

Any other speed of vibration will produce frequencies that misalign us... or put us in the state of what is known as our FalseSELF.

Gradually, we lose proper connection (alignment) with our TrueSelf by practicing the Thoughts, Attitudes, and Behaviors, which are not in agreement with our TrueSelf, thereby compromising (removing us from) our proper frequency.

This takes places because of the things that we introduce into our Mental State, that are NOT compatible with our TrueSELF frequency. This includes basic lifestyle choices in our diet, standard social modeling, value system, etc.

To properly innerstand what's being expressed, let's briefly look at these ***three simple things.***

ONE

ENERGY = SELF/the Metaphysical You

TrueSELF = You when properly aligned

FalseSELF = You when misaligned

Example: Let's say that…

You playing basketball = Energy

You playing basketball in football gear = FalseSELF

You playing basketball in basketball gear = TrueSELF

There is only one you, this is like SELF (also like Energy). Because there is ONLY one actual outfit designed specifically for basketball, that's like TrueSelf (also like EMotion). Then all of the other outfits besides the type specifically for basketball would be FalseSELF (also like feelings).

Now you can wear any outfit YOU CHOOSE, but specifically outfit-wise, ONLY THIS IS CORRECT… just as ONLY that ONE specific frequency will have and keep you aligned with TrueSelf. Some outfits may come strikingly close… but they are still not exacting.

*(Group/individual PEP. List/say "inappropriate" outfits). *

TWO

So, now that we have begun to piece the puzzle together and see just **HOW ENERGY REALIGNS YOU/U (H.E.R.U).**

For the purpose of this DASOLAMI *PEP* (Personal Empowerment Process), we want to make it clear that when we refer to Energy as it relates to yourSELF, we are talking about your thought perception!!!

When we refer to Vibration we typically mean the thoughts you focus most on.

When we speak of frequenc(ies), we are referring to EVERYTHING in existence that affects or is affected by your thoughts.

(option for a group PEP)

The Door, the Window, a cherry, the wind, a sound, a drop of water, a hair, a breath, a sunray, a heartbeat, a look, a smile, a frown, a sneeze, a whistle, a cough, a tear, a feeling, etc, EVERYTHING is its own particular unique frequency.

(PEP. Have group name things that are frequencies)

THREE

ALL FREQUENCIES can be changed by simply changing the speed of their vibration.

It's simple,

change the vibration...

change the frequency.

A Door is only that door because of the rate/speed of the Energy's vibration making it to be the frequency that it is. As you change the frequency of that door, that door will begin the change.

Example

By adding the frequency of fire to the door you can change the frequency of (burn) the door into the frequency of ashes.

The same for water. When you change liquid water into ice, all you are doing is changing the vibration of the water, which changes its frequency, thus it becomes "a different type of thing". The same when you thaw out ice, or heat water to steam.

The same hold true for everything in existence except Tachiyon.

Have you spotted the common denominator yet? □

No? Ok, well it's other frequencies.

It takes another/other frequencies to change a frequency.

FEELings are frequencies, this shows us that it takes one or more FEELings to CHANGE A PARTICULAR FEELing.

There is A KEY factor at play though.

Perspective.

The original Thought(s) has to be infused with perspective. That determines what "role" the frequency will take on at the core of its manifestation.

In other words, you are NOT just sending out baseless/irrelevant Emotion, but Emotion that is Energy vibrating on a specific (conscious) perspective.

This simple hidden metaphysical truth is key to P.E.P (Personal Empowerment Process), the **very premise of HOW ENERGY REALIGNS YOU/U.**

You are the author, producer and star of your life's script.

You choose your roll in how it unfolds

Your life will ONLY BE the way that YOU PERCEIVE it to be.

YOU CHOOSE your life to be a particular way through your T.A.B

THINK of your ...THOUGHTS as Energy, ATTITUDE as Vibration, BEHAVIOR as frequency

Your **THOUGHTS** determines your ATTITUDE,

and your **ATTITUDE** dictates

your **BEHAVIOR**

So, it's up to you to keep T.A.B's on yourSELF...

(PEP. Some examples of TABs from the group/individual).

YOU CHOOSE *every* FEELing you've had, do and ever will have

Your EMotion, is simply that, your Energy in motion, originating at the point of TrueSelf, and moving along a spectrum containing ALL FEELings known and unknown. You decide which feeling(s) you want your EMotion (energy) to engage on this spectrum.

You choose joy, pain, pleasure, worry, hate, mistrust, fear, anger, happiness, compassion, etc., it's all YOUR CHOOSING.

Example

You're having an average day, then while walking down the street you find $100, this makes you super happy!!! □

Same scenario

Except that a minute before you see the money, you receive a call of some extremely terrible news. Now when you find the $100, it doesn't make you happy.

Why is this??? □

Health-Wealth-Happiness comes *FROM you, NOT TO you.*

Innerstanding how to apply this perspective is very important. ***This knowledge is the key to your success.***

No matter what is happening in your life, you can ALWAYS CHOOSE how you perceive it.

Nothing makes you have any particular FEELing,

YOU CHOOSE to have that FEELing.

Things outside of yourSELF only effect you ***how*** YOU CHOOSE to allow them to, ***because*** YOU CHOOSE them to.

This metaphysical truth even filters on down to the "laws" of physics (the physical world).

People condition themselves to …

Sit in a 200+ degree sauna and NOT break a sweat,

Walk bare feet on broken glass without their feet being pierced,

Lay on a bed of razor sharp nails without their skin being pierced,

Skinny dip outside, in ice water, in winter weather and not get ill.

This process is typically known as ___Mind Over Matter (M.O.M),___ (remember to always respect, listen to and obey your M.O.M) □

This is to say that the reality of our life is only what we make it to be, according to the TABs that we set on it.

There is a fundamental principle of physics that explains that an atom APPEARS to be a single solid mass particle of energy, but is in fact, NOT!!!

In actuality, an atom is a particle having protons, neutrons, electrons, with an infinite spacing (waves) between them.

<u>And that only when the observer looks at an atom,
does it take a definite shape.</u>

This means that NOTHING is really solid, but that MATTER is really a wave of energy that takes its shape according to your observing/perceiving it.

This also is true in the case of our lives. Our T.A.B causes people, places and things to APPEAR as what we perceive them to be.

So, Keep T.A.Bs on yourSELF.

Make sure that your T.A.B (Thoughts, Attitude and Behavior)
is where it needs to be,
in order for you to be at the frequency of your TrueSelf.

Your Thoughts ultimately determine what frequency your life is on.
It's a scientific truth that Minor (so-called "negative") and Major (so-called
"positive") thoughts have widely different vibrations, producing vastly
different ranges of frequencies.

So, whenever you have a Thought which you gage to be on the Minor
frequency range of the spectrum,
do NOT continue to reinforce it with similar THINKing,
as it will transform into an Attitude
And eventually produce a behavior.

But instead use your knowledge of the Divine Design,
KNOWING that things do NOT happen TO you,
but rather FOR you, BECAUSE OF you.

This perception is key in INFUSING the PEP to be what it is without trying
to FORCE IT.

Then YOU CHOOSE the Major frequency that is the exact opposite of the
Minor frequency FEELing you had, and raise your EMotion to that other
frequency that YOU CHOOSE.

You do this by first *accepting* that things are the way they are by the Divine Design of *your THOUGHTS*.

Select a Major frequency that YOU CHOOSE to be on and empower it, by steadily promoting thoughts from the Major frequency range of the spectrum... so that it will become your attitude instead.

If you find yourSELF returning to the minor frequencies of the scale DON'T FORCE IT... INSTEAD INFUSE IT!!!

- Forcing it = Trying to *make thing(s)* change that are resisting us
- Infusing it = *Allowing thing(s)* to be, and changing our perspective of them.

Do not become frustrated and give up, but instead, simply continuously remind yourSELF that things are exactly as they should be, and continue to THINK positive thoughts from the Major frequency range of the Spectrum.

Know and accept that Divine Design CAN NOT and NEED NOT be changed by you. You simply NEED TO CHANGE YOUR PERCEPTION of how you view and relate to the workings of the Divine Design.

The universe will remain as it is, you simply NEED TO CHANGE YOUR PERCEPTION of how you perceive it in order to determine how you receive it.

THE STANDARD FUNCTION OF ENERGY IS FOR IT TO ATTRACT ITS LIKENESS.

We have been mainly taught that opposites attract, meaning that Energy manifests frequency that seeks out energy of its opposite frequency.

This Information is indeed true, however, this is NOT the standard.

This only happens in the case of an Energy frequency needing to balance itself out. When Tachiyon produces a frequency that becomes overabundant due to the presence of too much like frequency, it will begin to attract the frequency/thing which is its exact opposite; in order to stabilize/balance itself out.

Examples:

> Someone whom is poor at managing their money, will initially find themselves amongst other individuals whom are also poor at managing their own money.
>
> As this happening continues, the individual's money mismanagement frequency will eventually attract someone who is good or great at managing money. If not a person, the individual may find themselves in a living arrangement where they can only spend but so much money (such as, hospital, residential treatment program, prison, military, mental institution, etc.).

If this does not correct the behavior, their Tachiyon can then produce more drastic situations, such as, loss of income, frozen assets, siege of assets or finances, increased bills, potential evictions/foreclosures, debt, etc).

We may perceive these things as negative happenings, but in actually, they are NOT.
NOTHING in our lives happens *to us*, but instead EVERYTHING in our lives happens *for us, **because of us.***

There are no coincidences, accidents, mistakes, luck (good nor bad), errors or happenstance. EVERY SINGLE THING as a part of the Divine Design, is MEANT to happen.

The things that take place in our lives is merely our Tachiyon doing its natural function (job), which is to bring us into realignment with our TrueSELF, to retain our natural perfected state of Health-Wealth-Happiness.

THE MAJOR (Constructive/"positive")

And

MINOR (Destructive/"negative")

FREQUENCIES

*The following continuum of Major and Minor frequencies are NOT in any particular order of spectrum.

*In actuality, these frequencies are NOT divided into two distinct categories, but instead are ALL happening along one continuum. The short line drawn in the middle is just a helpful ideal to allow the Processee to better gage what part of [FREQUENCY SCALE] their frequency is located/vibrating on and correct it if need be.

*This spectrum continuum is NOT a linear paradigm as displayed here, but is actually a circular overlapping interconnectedness.

Major frequencies

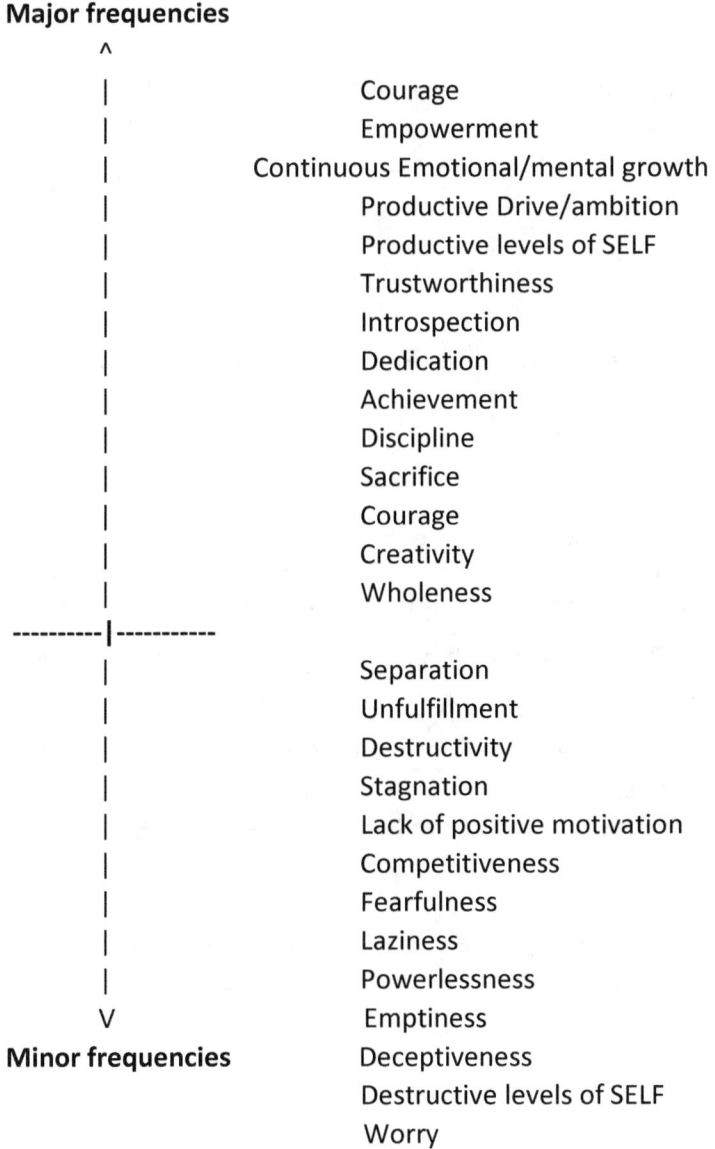

Courage
Empowerment
Continuous Emotional/mental growth
Productive Drive/ambition
Productive levels of SELF
Trustworthiness
Introspection
Dedication
Achievement
Discipline
Sacrifice
Courage
Creativity
Wholeness

Separation
Unfulfillment
Destructivity
Stagnation
Lack of positive motivation
Competitiveness
Fearfulness
Laziness
Powerlessness
Emptiness

Minor frequencies

Deceptiveness
Destructive levels of SELF
Worry

Carelessness
Solely artificial pleasure seeking.
Boredom
Need for constant entertainment
Usually distracted

These are just to present but a few of the major and minor frequencies.

NOTE:

The Productive levels of SELF would be, self-awareness, high self-esteem, self-love, self-respect, positive self-image, self-value/worth, self-motivation, self-realization, self-help, self-Empowerment, self-actualization, self-reliance, self-discipline, selflessness, etc, to highlight just a few.

The Destructive levels of SELF are, self-doubt, self-hatred, low self-esteem, poor self-image, self-destructiveness, etc, and all others which reflect the counter aspect of the Productive levels of SELF.

*(These two levels of SELF to be processed and discussed by the processee or group).

Minor frequency thought processes to be transformed:

No one ___ (likes me/cares about me/loves me, wants me).
She/He/People doesn't respect me.
It doesn't matter who I have to hurt, as long as I'm satisfied.
My life is messed up/crap/worthless, etc.
I am worthless/hopeless/useless/a failure/a loser/etc).
Something will go wrong, it always does.
Me, me, me.
I will never be able to do that.
S/he is better than me.
I don't care.
Why try.
It's useless/hopeless.
I don't trust anyone.
Poor me.
I always get a bad deal.
Survival of the fittest/only the strong survive.
Better them/her/him than me.
I don't care about anyone but myself.
I have to "get mine" (be successful) no matter what.
It's too hard.
I'm am not worth it.
You have to die from something.
I wish I were dead.
No one cares about me.
Life is too hard.
I'm not good enough.
Nothing ever goes my way.
The world is against me.

The world would be better off without me.

I can't do it.

I'm not (good, smart, skilled, attractive, deserving, etc) enough.

My way or the highway.

It's too hard (I don't want to try).

I will never amount to anything.

I hate ___. (anything) Them/her/him/it/life/you/myself/this ___ (place, feeling, etc)

Why should I change?

Everyone else has the problem, not me.

Life is a struggle.

I'm not going to suffer alone.

I don't deserve _____. (it/her/him/them/that/etc).

*Just to present a few.

If you recognize ANY of these TAB frequencies in yourSELF, begin immediately to process them by acknowledging them as Minor frequency processes, and applying the opposite Thought process from the Major frequency range. If you are a Processor, have the processee address these Minor frequency TABs.

YOUR CHOICE, YOUR VOICE

(You have a choice in every situation)

The Grand Model

View yourSELF (Energy) as an architect and landlord of your life
You design a building = ALL of the people, places, things, happenings and circumstances throughout your entire life.

YOU DECIDE what the building will be, (apartment, office or something altogether different). YOU DECIDE how many floors, the height, width, depth and working components of the building.
Just as YOU CHOOSE/design everything in your entire life.
As the landlord/owner, it is your responsibility to manage it. Just as it is your responsibly to manage your life in all its aspects.
Each floor = a frequency
The things, events & people on each floor = The people and things that occupy that particular frequency permanently or temporarily.
You going from floor to floor = Emotion
You choose which floor (feeling(s)) you go to (have).

You, as the architect, design the building (your life) ACCORDING TO PERCEPTION (how you interpret things to be or needing to be).

1) The Lesser models

You decide to color with markers
Think of a package of markers which contains every color

You are The Energy
The package that the markers are in = Major/Minor frequency scale
Each color marker in the package = A specific feeling/frequency
You deciding on a specific color = Perception
The Process of you physically selecting that color = Emotion

The CHOICE of marker used to color the picture is typically influenced by…

- WHAT THE PICTURE IS
- HOW YOU SEE THE PICTURE
- THE COLORS YOU LIKE…

All of those things are contingent on OUR PERCEPTION

2)

You decide to get dressed for the day

You = energy
Where you keep your clothes = Major/Minor frequency scale
All of your clothes = feelings/frequencies
Deciding what to wear = Perception
Process of physically selecting your outfit = Emotion

You will select your outfit according to YOUR PERCEPTION of how you want to look.

We have to SAFEGUARD our THINKing at ALL TIMES.
Only feed yourSELF with positive THOUGHTS. As *you do this more,* the more *easily and naturally this will work for you.*

Identifying with the FalseSELF image of ourselves that has been selected for us, and by us, misaligns us from our *TrueSelf.* This disrupts our chance of obtaining our normal state of **Health-Wealth-Happiness.**

Therefore seek out ONLY that which aligns you with your TrueSelf.

Conclusion

There is but *one Energy* source, and ITS vibration creates and sustains *ALL ELSE*, seen and unseen.

Every single thing in existence, including us, are but mere "Energy *expressions"* (expressions of THAT Energy). In other words, we are THAT Energy, purposely "removed" from ITSELF by ITSELF in order to objectively experience ITSELF.

And because we are "removed" from that Energy, but this Energy created and sustains us, we are compelled to seek remnants of that Energy within *everything and everyone*, and intake doses of IT when, where and however we can.

This additional need for excess Energy is the basis for *Repetitive Dynamic Cycles* and *Redundant Drama Skits,* the most damaging factors hindering us from realigning with our TrueSelf.

``

Repetitive Dynamic Cycle (RDC)

A negative ritualistic vampiric behavioral technique, which people use on themselves and/or others, based on the manipulative intention of extorting Energy from the target(s).

HOW THE RITUAL WORKS – Initiator of rite presents some major or minor issue(s), (whether real or imaged, self-created or by another, theirs or someone else's) that's never presented for the purpose of having a productive overcome, but only to draw the participant(s) actively and willingly (whether consciously or unconsciously) into the issue, for the purpose of feeding off of the participants' Energy.

It is referred to as repetitive because this behavioral technique is done repeatedly... only to different targets each time.

Redundant drama skit (RDS)

This is *extremely similar* to a *RDC*, except in that this one is based on a *familiar or identical* issue(s) played out *over and over again* between *the same* participant(s).

*A RDC is a specific issue that one targets people universally with.

*A RDS is a specific issue that one goes through repeatedly with a specific person/people

Both of these can be done on oneself as well as on another/others.

More on RDCs and RDSs, in the next booklets

Happy Process of H.E.R.U